ALEXANDER PUSHKIN

Mozart and Salieri

THE LITTLE TRAGEDIES

Antony Wood's translations from Russian have
appeared in anthologies published by Penguin and
in *Stand* magazine; some of his translations of
Pushkin were performed at the Cheltenham
Festival of Literature in 1981; his version of *Mozart
and Salieri* was performed in autumn 1982 on BBC
Radio 3 by Paul Scofield and Simon Callow, and
his *Stone Guest* was a BBC commission.

Cover of Pushkin's manuscript 'Dramatic Scenes', 1830

ALEXANDER PUSHKIN

Mozart and Salieri

THE LITTLE TRAGEDIES
translated by
ANTONY WOOD

Foreword by Elaine Feinstein

ANGEL BOOKS
LONDON

For Hazel and Jessica

First published in Great Britain 1982 by
Angel Books, 3 Kelross Road, London N5 1RF

ISBN 0 946162 02 6 (cased)
0 946162 00 X (paper)

*Printed in England by Skelton's Press Ltd.
Wellingborough, Northamptonshire.*

Contents

Acknowledgements

This book would not have been completed as soon as it was, or perhaps ever, without the encouragement and enthusiasm of Piers Plowright, who produced *Mozart and Salieri* and *The Stone Guest* for Radio 3. These two versions have benefited greatly from his auditory sensitivity. I am also very grateful to Kitty Mrosovsky, James Greene, Tony Briggs and my wife Hazel for their critical scrutiny of successive drafts.

Foreword

by Elaine Feinstein

It was in the wild hymn of praise that Pushkin gives to
Walsingham in *The Feast during the Plague* that Marina
Tsvetayeva* found the most powerful example of genius
abandoning ordinary morality. As far as I know, this short
play has never been available in translation before in this
country. For that reason alone, we might be grateful to
Antony Wood for this volume of Pushkin's *Little Tragedies*.
In fact, each of the pieces has its own fascination; especially,
perhaps, *Mozart and Salieri,* which turns on Salieri's
motivation, but contains an intriguing portrait of Mozart
too. To my reading, not all of *The Miserly Knight* matches the
grandeur of the Baron's famous soliloquy. But these *Little
Tragedies* are not so much plays as sketches, which imply the
drama behind them. In taking only dramatic high-points,
they offer what the critic Mirsky has described as 'the
application to drama of the lyrical method . . .' At the word
'lyrical' the English reader who has previously been
disappointed by translations of Pushkin may well draw
back. The very qualities which make Pushkin so much a
miracle when read in Russian have usually made him
singularly intractable to translation. But here, perhaps
because the inspiration of these pieces was so very much
English, perhaps because Pushkin experiments in them
with the use of a blank verse alien to the Russian tradition,
Antony Wood has succeeded admirably in making these
dramatic poems accessible to us all.

*In the essay 'Art in the Light of Conscience'.

Introduction

To the Russians, Pushkin is a miracle. His was the hand that transformed a lumbering carthorse of a language into a literary Pegasus. He was the final shaper of a language that has remained intact from his day to this, and that the modern schoolboy, taxi-driver, writer and engineer takes as his own. He fits the syntax and natural rhythms of Russian to metre as music to the barline. His is a Popian balanced precision allied to Romantic and modern feeling; infinite stylistic variety to suit literary purpose; diction that links the most trivial colloquial phrase with charged utterance in one continuous spectrum – that exalts, indeed, everyday life to poetry.

Pushkin laid the foundations of what the world knows as Russian literature, in numerous genres: narrative poems, tragic and comic; lyrics and other short poems; dramatic verse, fairy tales in verse, a novel in verse; prose tales long and short; a number of pregnant fragments; letters, criticism and historical writings. His achievement was a literary parallel to Peter the Great's: he too led Russia into Europe.

The *Little Tragedies* are his most original contribution to drama – far more effective in their way than the historical tragedy *Boris Godunov* at which he worked so carefully, in such high hopes of creating a tradition of Shakespearean drama in Russia. They also contain some of his finest poetry. He completed the four pieces in blank verse in the autumn of 1830, confined, shortly before his marriage, to his newly acquired country estate at Boldino, Nizhny Novgorod by an outbreak of cholera, for three of the most productive months of his life. Comparatively late in his verse output – written after *Eugene Onegin*, most of the lyrics and narrative poems, and *Boris Godunov*, at a moment when his public, and he himself, was turning away from verse to prose – the *Little Tragedies* exemplify, in many ways, Pushkin's essential qualities. *Mozart and Salieri* was his only dramatic work to be staged in his lifetime (twice in 1832); *The Miserly Knight* was within three days of its première when he died and the production was cancelled. *The Stone Guest* was the only one of the four pieces not published in his lifetime; the others appeared variously in the course of the 1830s.

As with *Boris*, English inspiration played its part in the genesis of the *Little Tragedies*. In 1829 Pushkin read the *Dramatic Scenes* of Barry Cornwall (pseudonym of Bryan Procter, 1787-1874) in a volume published in the original in Paris the same year. Procter was a fashionable man of letters who numbered Byron, Keats, Leigh Hunt and Charles Lamb among his friends. His *Dramatic Scenes* in blank verse presented climaxes without exposition or development, revelling in the heightened emotional moment and the grand speech. They were written for a public that had acquired a taste for Shakespearean tragedy and the acting of Edmund Kean. In them Pushkin at last found a form in which to treat certain dramatic subjects he had noted down several years before.

Procter begins his foreword to the *Dramatic Scenes*, in the 1829 edition: 'One object that I had in view, when I wrote these "Scenes", was to try the effect of a more natural style than that which has for a long time prevailed in our dramatic literature. I have endeavoured to mingle poetical imagery with expressions of natural emotion: but it has been my wish, where the one seemed to jar with the other, that the former should give place to the latter. In this spirit I have ventured to let several passages, little interesting perhaps otherwise than as a representation of human dialogue, remain.' In the *Little Tragedies*, which significantly develop the genre essayed by Procter beyond his achievement, Pushkin accomplishes to perfection the mingling of 'poetical imagery with expressions of natural emotion'; the language of poetry consorts unjarringly with the language of everyday, in contrast or in fusion.

One of Pushkin's draft titles for the pieces was 'Dramatic Investigations', before he decided on the less explicit title; and he describes them as 'dramatic sketches, dramatic studies, an essay in dramatic studies'. Each focuses on a single theme or situation: the clash between a miser and his impecunious son in *The Miserly Knight*; the impact of uncontrollable genius on common humanity in *Mozart and Salieri*; Don Juan's return from exile to his old haunts and habits, and his fatal meeting with the statue of the Comendador, in *The Stone Guest*; and most starkly of all, a single scene of carousal by desperate survivors of the Black Death in *The Feast during the Plague*. The *Little Tragedies* explore the psychological moment, each starting shortly before the wave breaks, bringing the action to a head after brief enactment of the precipitatory stages. The shortest is a mere two hundred lines, the longest a mere five hundred. The literary historian Prince Mirsky has called them 'dramatic "points" . . . charged with such significance that they do not demand any further development', 'the application to drama of the lyrical method of concentration'.*

Although these pieces have striking dramatic qualities, they would seem to have been written to be read rather than staged; and indeed, though they continue to be staged from time to time, evidence of their success as stage drama is lacking. Mirsky's emphasis on the idea of 'concentration' indicates an essential difference between dramatic sketches and full-scale drama. It could be that radio is the most effective means of realising the *Little Tragedies*.

Their blank verse is of a kind unprecedented and unparalleled in Russian, dispensing with the regular caesura of *Boris Godunov*, moving with a free swing, an abundance of enjambement, riding the contours of the Russian language. Salieri's two soliloquies, and the Baron's in *The Miserly Knight*, are mighty peaks in Russian blank verse, the latter occupying a place in the national memory equivalent to that of, say, 'To be or not to be' in the English.

*D. S. Mirsky, *A History of Russian Literature*, edited by F. J. Whitfield, Alfred A. Knopf, New York, 1949.

John Bayley has written of these speeches, Salieri's first soliloquy based on the inexorable, step-by-step unfolding of logical argument, and the Baron's so powerfully creating his imaginative world: 'Acting at once as apologia and exposition, they both reveal the speaker and embody him, making audible in his words a whole background of history and culture. The Baron is a figure in the foreground of a huge canvas, portraying court and camp, swarming armies and seascapes, grandees in satin and beggars in rags. Salieri's speech is like a feat of classical architecture, a structure massive and elegant, whose symmetry is both severe and self-absorbed. Their tone determines the shape and body of each drama, giving it the compact unity which is the secret of the genre as Pushkin developed it, and far removed from the insipid freedom of the scenes he found in Barry Cornwall.'*

Pushkin's subtitle for the first of the Little Tragedies to be completed, *The Miserly Knight* – 'Scenes from Chenstone's tragi-comedy *The Covetous Knight*' – is probably a device to conceal his authorship; there seems to be no work of this title by the eighteenth-century English poet William Shenstone (mis-spelled by Pushkin) – though certain ideas and images are taken from Shenstone's poem *Economy. A Rhapsody, Addressed to Young Poets*. Pushkin's father was something of a miser, and he describes in a letter an incident of some similarity to that with which *The Miserly Knight* ends: he presumably did not wish his father to be thought a model for the Baron.

In the *Little Tragedies* as elsewhere in his works, Pushkin gives human depth to the central characters. Whilst it could hardly be claimed that any character in the *Little Tragedies* is a 'rounded human being', the protagonists are a good deal more than types. Thus the miserly Baron is not just the epitome of miserliness, like Molière's Harpagon; nor is he confined to characteristics derived from mammon, such as the lawlessness of a Volpone. The Baron is possessed with

*John Bayley, *Pushkin: A Comparative Commentary*, Cambridge University Press, 1971.

the idea of power; he enjoys it in imagination; knowing that money equals power, he is content to *know* his power rather than exercise it. But he is also proud of his status as a knight, and is staunchly faithful to his liege-lord the Duke; and his capitalist instincts leave room for valuation of human feelings. His son Albert, whom he keeps in his house in poverty, has every incentive to hasten his inheritance, yet is horrified at the suggestion that he might achieve this by poisoning his father (as a knight, however, he is quite ready to kill his father in duel). Another 'humanising' touch: Pushkin actually gives Albert, clearly an aggrieved party deserving of sympathy, an element of the ridiculous on his first appearance. The young knight is so impoverished that any loss or damage to his equipment is a disaster, and he reveals that his astonishing courage at tournament sprang entirely from fury over a ruined helmet.

Mozart and Salieri was the second of the *Little Tragedies* to be completed. Pushkin read details of Mozart's life in various sources of the day, and he knew of the well-publicised Gluck-Piccini 'rivalry' in Paris in the 1770s. Two years after writing *Mozart and Salieri* he noted the following: 'During the first performance of *Don Giovanni*, while the audience, overwhelmed, was drinking in Mozart's harmonies in silence, a loud whistle was heard. Everybody turned round in amazement and indignation; the famous Salieri left the hall, consumed by mad envy. Salieri died about eight years ago. Some German journals wrote that he confessed, on his deathbed, to having committed a terrible crime; he had poisoned the great Mozart. A man driven by envy to whistle at *Don Giovanni* would have been capable of poisoning its creator.'*

Antonio Salieri, six years Mozart's senior, appointed court composer and conductor of the Italian opera in Vienna at the age of twenty-four, was one of the most powerful musical figures of his day; a popular composer of opera, friend of Haydn and Gluck, and teacher of

*Quoted by V. Terras, Introduction to *The Little Tragedies* (in Russian), Bradda Books, Letchworth, 1966; the quotation is here edited by A.W.

Beethoven, Schubert and Liszt. His worldly career was infinitely more successful than Mozart's. The deathbed 'confession' he is reported to have made would seem to have been entirely without foundation, but in Pushkin's time controversy over the matter was sharp: Salieri's defenders argued mental derangement, and in Russia one poet attacked *Mozart and Salieri* on the grounds of factual misrepresentation. Be all this as it may, and whilst Pushkin's knowledge of Mozart's life was scant enough for him to portray the composer finishing his Requiem, his grasp of the nature of Mozart's genius is altogether more sure – perhaps because it bore some resemblance to his own.

Mozart and Salieri is a study in motivation. The light-hearted, quicksilver unpredictability of genius is set against the plodding, painstaking doggedness of mere talent. We are shown envy at work, but Salieri's conscious mind works up 'rational' arguments in demonstration of the idea that to poison his friend will be an act of justice furthering the cause of art – by for example protecting the general community of artists from being reduced to worthlessness by Mozart's genius. The working out of Salieri's motivation, at conscious and unconscious levels, is cogent, all the more so because Salieri's destructive envy consorts with real fondness for Mozart, and reverence for his art. To Salieri goes most of the poetry, whilst Mozart's is the utterance of everyday; the two levels of language are in marked contrast. Salieri's poetry movingly expresses his predicament; a musical genius has no need of fine words – though Mozart does have some to say.

In *The Stone Guest* Pushkin sets his own very individual conception of Don Juan against the tradition of the 'heartless and impious seducer' first given literary form by the seventeenth-century Spanish dramatist Gabriel Tellez (Tirso de Molina) in *El Burlador de Sevilla,* a play that Pushkin may have known, though we are more certain that he was familiar with Molière's *Don Juan* and Mozart's *Don Giovanni* (his epigraph is taken from the latter). Pushkin's Don Juan is a very different figure from those of earlier treatments. He is sensitive to women as individuals, appreciative of male qualities too, and gifted with poetic eloquence; at the same time, his behaviour is traditional. Pushkin's is the only version of the story in which Doña Anna is the wife of the Comendador, giving rise to retrospective sexual jealousy in Don Juan, who seeks to humiliate his dead 'rival' by inviting his statue to stand guard outside his widow's house while he himself makes free within. And we learn that in the fight with the Comendador, Don Juan was not the aggressor.

We see Don Juan in three successive modes of love, in the first two wholly natural and at ease: in tender reminiscence of the dead Iñez, then in robust reunion with the young actress Laura, a female counterpart of himself. Finally, he is the virtuoso wooer of Doña Anna, seemingly the type of the bourgeois widow, but who begins to crumble under his assault before the dénouement.

Don Juan remains a complex, elusive figure – the seriousness of his love for Doña Anna has long been debated among readers of the piece – yet we have glimpses, in some of the qualities above-mentioned, of a living human being. And three other characters (not counting Leporello, who is the familiar figure from *Don Giovanni*) receive individual definition in the short compass of the play: the sensually exuberant young actress Laura; her gloomy lover Carlos; and the biddable Doña Anna. Even the statue of the Comendador has personal responses: he shows anger in the scene with Don Juan and Leporello; and is there a touch of jealousy on his side too, when he says to Don Juan at the end: 'Leave her. All is finished'? Pushkin enacts legend in terms of human beings.

Anna Akhmatova, in an article published in 1958, drew attention to the autobiographical content of *The Stone Guest*. (It might here be worth remembering the autobiographical element in *The Miserly Knight* – and in *The Feast during the Plague* too, in the cholera outbreak, reminiscent of the time of the Plague, during which the *Little Tragedies* were completed.) Akhmatova admits a strong autobiographical element to her reading of *The Stone Guest*, the gist of which, from this point of view, F. F. Seeley has thus summarised:

'Pushkin, at this time – on the eve of his marriage – is haunted by a fear or foreboding of retribution: having played the Don Juan himself till now, he is about to find himself in the role of Don Alvaro, i.e. set to guard the honour of a young and beautiful wife against her own inexperience and the arts of other, younger Don Juans. He realises that this may cost him his life (as in fact happened) and, although he is not afraid to die, he is afraid to have happiness snatched from him, and, worse, to leave his wife a young and brilliant widow free to remarry as she chooses. Natalya [Pushkin's wife], like Anna, is marrying without love, at her mother's bidding. "And so in the tragedy *The Stone Guest* Pushkin is punishing himself – his younger, carefree, sinful self, and the theme of vengeance from beyond the grave (i.e. fear of such) is heard no less loudly than the theme of retribution."'*

The language of *The Stone Guest* fits the broad dramatic treatment. The colloquial and the sublime are fused, the one giving way to, indeed *becoming,* the other, where in the course of ordinary conversation utterance is suddenly heightened: Don Juan's reverie on Iñez, for example, Carlos's speech to Laura about old age, even a mere three lines or so on love from the First Guest. The work takes us to the core of Pushkin's poetry, founded, in John Bayley's phrase, in 'a language realising the full potential of its simplest words'.

The last of the *Little Tragedies* to be completed, *The Feast during the Plague,* is a translation of part of a scene from John Wilson's *The City of the Plague,* first published in 1816 and reissued in 1829 in the composite volume which also introduced Pushkin to Barry Cornwall's *Dramatic Scenes*. Here is a classic case of literary alchemy. Pushkin selects a pregnant moment from Wilson's rambling three-act (melo)drama in blank verse, with highpoints provided by two songs and a confrontation between priest and revellers; he polishes and prunes (sometimes severely), recreates the two songs with

*F. F. Seeley, 'The Problem of *Kamennyy Gost*'', *Slavonic and East European Review,* XLI, 97, June 1963. This article discusses romantic and anti-romantic views of Don Juan's wooing of Doña Anna.

almost entirely fresh material – and transforms his original into a self-contained, hauntingly eloquent scene, whose central character, Walsingham, Master of the Revels, is as possessed a figure as any of the protagonists of the *Little Tragedies*. Here the preoccupation with death already evident in the three original *Little Tragedies,* especially *The Stone Guest* in which Don Juan baits death with toreador-like impudence, is overt and central. In her beautiful lament, the Scottish prostitute Mary views the Plague-stricken world with feminine sensibility; Walsingham's song in celebration of the Plague is a majestic expression of the exhilaration found in life under threat of death.

In translating Pushkin's translation 'back into English', I have gone a little further in his own reductive direction, while using words and phrases from Wilson where they seemed stylistically apt (for example, the opening two lines); and keeping Pushkin's creative mistranslations. It has of course been my intention to preserve, in spirit and in style, Pushkin's distance from Wilson. So that the reader may judge for himself the relationship between my version of Pushkin and his original, the relevant part of Wilson's *The City of the Plague*, Act I, Scene iv is included in this book as an Appendix.

The Baron, Salieri, Don Juan, Walsingham – all are dreamers immersed in their private, inner worlds, pursuing their obsessions to a point of furthest remove from outer reality and the social code, meeting their downfall with the nemesis of reality. For the Baron, such a moment comes in the clash with his son to whom he has denied livelihood in the indulgence of his reveries of power; for Salieri, with the growing realisation that the immortality of genius can never be his, and that far from being a servant of art he is its destroyer; for Don Juan, with the death that he mocks, or courts; whilst Walsingham, taking the Black Death as life-enhancing, might be viewed as frozen at such a moment throughout, embodying the split between inner and outer worlds in the most extreme degree of all. For all these extraordinary figures, Pushkin wins our fascinated sympathy.

I have aimed to render Pushkin in the language of today, but not sounding exactly as if it had been written today; too pointedly current an idiom would I feel have resulted in too great a seachange for a writer with roots in the eighteenth century. The polysyllabic rhythms of Russian are unfortunately quite impossible to capture in English translation: in keeping to the overall syllabic count of Pushkin's blank verse, I have allowed the loss of syllables in English to result in fewer lines than in the original. At the same time I have tried to express as often as possible effects such as alliteration, repetition, word placement and enjambement. It has been my endeavour to keep the original firmly in sight, and to achieve versions that work as English verse.

A.W.

The Miserly Knight

SCENE I

Inside a tower. Albert and Ivan.

ALBERT

I must be at the Tournament today,
Cost what it will. My helmet, Ivan.

Ivan hands him his helmet.

                                        Pierced
Quite through. How can I ever wear it now?
I need a new one. Damned Delorges!

IVAN

                              But then
You paid him back! After you knocked him flying
He lay all day half-dead – and after that
He scarcely mended.

ALBERT

                        Still, his armour's whole;
His new Venetian breastplate wasn't damaged;
As for his breast, no loss to him on that –
He'll not be put to purchasing another.
Why did I not relieve him of his helmet?
I would have had it off him, but for shame
Before the Duke and ladies. Damned Delorges!
If only he'd run through my head. Also
I need some clothes. Last time, when all the knights
Sat in their silk and velvet, only I
Appeared in cuirass at the Duke's grand table.
I had to say I'd come that day by chance.
What shall I say this time? O poverty!
How it humiliates the heart! – When, now,
Delorges's heavy lance thrust through my helmet
And I, with head uncovered, turned and spurred
My Emir on to catch him like a whirlwind
And hurled him from the saddle twenty paces
As if he were a page; and all the ladies
Rose from their seats as one, and even Clothilda

Could not hold back a cry, and hid her face;
And all the heralds trumpeted my stroke –
What lay behind the bravery of that deed,
And such prodigious strength, was known to none!
Rage at a ruined helmet – simply that
That prompted those heroics; miserliness . . .
Sharing a roof with such a father as mine,
You can't avoid infection. How's poor Emir?

IVAN

Still lame. He's not for riding.

ALBERT

                    Well, so be it,
I'll have to buy the bay. He won't cost much.

IVAN

Not much? We haven't any money at all!

ALBERT

What says the good-for-nothing Solomon?

IVAN

No more from him without security.

ALBERT

Security! And where the Devil find it?

IVAN

That's what I told him.

ALBERT

            And – ?

IVAN

                    He hummed and ha'ed.

ALBERT

You said I have a father as rich as he is,
And one day I'll inherit all?

IVAN

                    I said so.

ALBERT

And then?

IVAN

He hummed and ha'ed again.

ALBERT

                                        Ye gods!

IVAN

He said he'd come and see you.

ALBERT

                              That's more like it.
I'll keep him here – he'll have to pay a ransom.

Knocking at the door.

Who's there?

Enter Jew.

JEW

Your humble servant.

ALBERT

                                   Ah, my friend!
Accursèd Jew – Most honoured Solomon –
Come in, I pray: now what is this I hear –
You don't believe in credit?

JEW

                         Gracious Knight,
Believe me, gladly I would . . . I truly cannot.
Where would I find the money? Helping knights
Has ruined me. No one pays. I meant to ask –
If I could have the first instalment . . .

ALBERT

                                   Robber!
Would I be bothered with you if I had money?
Don't be so obstinate, my Solomon:
Let's have those ducats. Count me out a hundred,
Before I have you searched.

JEW

                         A hundred ducats!
If only I had a hundred ducats!

ALBERT

                    Listen –
Aren't you ashamed to turn away old friends?

JEW

I swear . . .

ALBERT

          Enough. You want security?
Now what security could I give you –
A pigskin? Had I a single thing to pawn,
I'd long ago have pawned it. So, my word,
My word as knight, you dog, will not suffice?

JEW

Your word, good sir, while you're alive, means much:
A magic key to all the wealth of Flanders.
But give it to the likes of me, and then
(The Lord forbid) you were to die – your word
Would serve me every bit as well as, say,
The key to some old casket lost at sea.

ALBERT

It cannot be I shan't outlive my father!

JEW

Who knows? For who can reckon up his days?
The youth that blooms today is dead tomorrow,
And withered shoulders bear him to the grave.
The Baron's healthy: God may grant he'll live
Ten, twenty years, or twenty-five, or thirty.

ALBERT

Nonsense! In thirty years, Jew, I'll be fifty,
And then – what earthly need for money?

JEW

                              Money? –
Money will serve the needs of any age:
The young man seeks in it a nimble servant
To speed about the world and do his bidding;
An old man sees in it a faithful friend
To cherish like the pupil of his eye.

ALBERT

My father sees it not as friend or servant,
But master – serves it like some Eastern slave,
A dog upon a chain. He lives in squalor,
He lights no fire, and feeds on crusts and water;
He never sleeps at night, but runs and barks –
The gold it is that sleeps. No more of this!
One day I'll be the master of that gold:
That day it shall not sleep.

JEW
                              Ah yes indeed,
Upon the Baron's funeral-day we'll see
More money flow than tears. May bounteous God
Hasten your due inheritance.

ALBERT
                              Amen!

JEW
You could now . . .

ALBERT
                    What?

JEW
                              There is a way I've thought of .

ALBERT
A way?

JEW
          I know an old apothecary,
A Jew, in poverty . . .

ALBERT
                    A usurer
Like you – rather more honest, though, I hope?

JEW
No sir, Old Tovy's is another trade –
Potions . . . They work quite wonderfully.

ALBERT
                                        Potions?

JEW

Three drops in water – colourless, no taste –
No stomach pains or sickness . . . and you die.

ALBERT

A trafficker in poison!

JEW

Yes, in poison.

ALBERT

What's this? Instead of money you will lend
So many phials of poison at a ducat?

JEW

Laugh at me if you wish. I thought perhaps . . .
The Baron's time had come . . .

ALBERT

What do I hear?
A father to be poisoned by his son!
How dare he . . . Ivan, hold him! Jewish dog –
Snake of a Jew! I'll hang you from the gatepost!

JEW

Forgive a jest, sir!

ALBERT

Ivan, come – a rope!

JEW

I spoke in jest – in jest! I've brought you money.

ALBERT

Out of my sight, you dog!

Exit Jew.

My father's avarice –
What has it driven me to! This wretched Jew,
How could he dare . . . Get me a glass of wine,
I'm trembling . . . Ivan, how I need that money.
After that Jew, and bring me back his ducats!
My inkwell, quickly. Now – I'll write the swindler
A note of pledge. Don't let me see him again,

That Judas . . . Ah, they'll smell of poison, like
The silver pieces of his ancestor . . .
I asked for wine!

IVAN

We've not a drop.

ALBERT

                                    The gift

From Spain?

IVAN

              Last night we gave the end of it
To that sick smith.

ALBERT

                Oh yes . . . Some water then.
This life! My mind's made up. I'll see the Duke
And seek redress from him: he'll force my father
To keep me like a son, not like a mouse
Down in the cellar.

SCENE II

A cellar.

THE BARON

Like a young buck who waits aflame to keep
His assignation with some profligate
Or helpless innocent, so I have waited
Long hours for this the moment I behold
In secret, in my cellar, these true coffers.
O happy day! Into the sixth of them,
Not filled yet to the brim, today I'll drop
Another handful of new-gathered gold.
Little it seems, but riches grow
Little by little. Once, I read, a tsar
Ordered his men to pile up earth in handfuls;
A proud hill soon arose, and from its summit

The tsar was wont, it seems, to feast his eyes
Upon the valleys clad with gleaming tents,
Upon the sea alive with speeding ships.
In handfuls too, I've carried to this cellar
Regular tribute, here I've raised my hill –
And view my wide dominion. What is not
Subject to me, to my demonic rule?
At my desiring, palaces will rise,
And nymphs come dancing through my splendid gardens;
The muses will compete to bring me tribute,
Genius abandon liberty, my slave,
Virtue and never-resting labour humbly
Await their due reward from me. I'll whistle,
And shyly blood-stained crime will creep to me,
And lick my hand, and look into my eyes
To read in them some signal of my will.
All things submit to me, and I to nothing;
I am above desire; I am at peace;
I know my power – all I need to know . . .

Gazes upon his gold.

Little it seems . . . Of what, in human care –
In tears, deceptions, curses, prayers – is it
The weighty representative! A widow
Repaid me with this old doubloon today . . .
Well I remember her from years ago,
Upon her knees all day outside my window
Weeping, with three small children by her side.
It rained, and stopped, began to rain again –
Never did that dissembler leave her place;
I could have had her driven away, but somehow
I sensed she had a husband's debt to pay,
And didn't wish to find herself in prison.
This – from an idle rascal . . . How could he
Have come by such a piece? Why, theft, of course,
Night robbery on the highway, in the forest . . .
If ever all the tears, the sweat and blood
Shed for the riches that are hoarded here
Broke on us from the bowels of the Earth –

There'd be a Second Flood, and I should drown
Deep in my faithful cellars. Now it's time.

Prepares to unlock a coffer.

Each time I stand before my gold, to open
A coffer, how I flush and tremble . . . not,
I think, from fear (who is there I should fear?
I have my sword: this faithful blade of mine
Shall answer for my gold) – My being is seized
By singular, unknown sensations . . . Doctors
Maintain that certain men find joy in killing.
Placing the key inside the lock, I feel
What men must feel who plunge the knife: both joy
And terror.

Unlocks the coffer.

Earthly bliss is here!

Puts in more coins.

So now,
Enough of chasing round the weary world
To serve the passions and the needs of men.
Here you shall sleep the sleep of strength and peace,
The sleep of gods amidst the depths of heaven . . .
Today shall be a feast-day: lighted candles
Shall stand before each open, brimming coffer,
And I shall gaze upon my glittering hoard.

Lights candles and opens the coffers one after another.

My kingdom lies before me! . . . Wondrous glitter!
A mighty realm, obedient to my rule;
My happiness, my honour and my glory!
My kingdom . . . Who shall be, though – after me –
The sovereign of it all? That son of mine!
That empty-headed wastrel of a son,
Who keeps companionship with rakes and rogues!
The moment I am dead, he'll come – beneath
These chaste and peaceful vaults he'll come, surrounded
With all his court of greedy hangers-on.
He'll rob my lifeless body of these keys,

He'll open every coffer with a laugh,
My gold will pour through holes in satin pockets;
He'll trample precious vessels underfoot,
He'll soak the dust with holy oil – he'll squander . . .
What right has he? Have I acquired all this
From fortune's hand, as lightly as a gambler
Rattling his dice and raking in his winnings?
Whoever could record the harsh privations,
Restraints of passion, weighty calculations,
And all the days of care and wakeful nights
My gold has cost? Or will my son maintain
My moss-grown heart has never known desire,
And conscience never gnawed my vitals, conscience,
The sharp-clawed beast that tears the heart out, conscience,
The uninvited guest, unloved companion,
Uncivil creditor – the awesome witch
That makes the moon grow dark, the grave, confounded,
Yield up its dead? . . . He who has gained his riches
Through suffering – see that poor unfortunate
Waste what was won with blood. Would I could hide
This cellar from unworthy eyes! Possess
The power to leave the grave, returning here
A watchful spirit seated on a coffer,
To guard, as now, my riches from the living!

SCENE III

The Duke's castle. Albert; the Duke.

ALBERT

The shame of bitter poverty, my lord,
Has long been mine. And were it not for dire
Necessity, you'd never hear my case.

THE DUKE

You speak the truth, I know: a noble knight
Would never stoop to accuse a father, should
The cause be not of dire extremity . . .

29

But have no fear; this matter shall be laid,
Alone with me, before your father's conscience.
I've sent for him. How long since last I saw him!
He used to be a close friend of my grandfather.
He'd seat me as a child upon his horse
And hold his heavy helmet over me
Like some enormous bell.

Looks out of the window.

Can this be him?

ALBERT

It is, my lord.

THE DUKE

This way. I'll call you.

Exit Albert. Enter the Baron.

Baron,
How glad I am to see you keep good health.

BARON

I'm happy, noble lord, I still have strength
To answer your command.

THE DUKE

How long, good sir,
Since last we met. Do you remember me?

BARON

As plainly as I see you now, my lord.
And what a child you were. The Duke your grandfather
Would say to me: 'Philip' (he always called me
Philip), 'In twenty years we'll both be fools
Beside this boy here.' You . . .

THE DUKE

Let us renew
Acquaintance. You're a stranger to my court.

BARON

I have grown old, my lord: what would I do
At court? You're young, and fond of tournaments
And banquets. I'm not fit for them. But then,

Should God grant war, I'd place my aching bones
Upon a horse once more, this trembling arm
Would yet have strength to draw a sword for you.

THE DUKE

Your ardour, Baron, well we know; my grandfather
And you were friends; my father honoured you.
I've always counted you a brave, true knight –
But let us sit. Do you have children, sir?

BARON

One son.

THE DUKE

      Why do I never see him? If
My court is not for you – his years and station
Would fit him well for it.

BARON

          He shuns the world;
His is a wild and sombre disposition –
He roams the forests like a stag.

THE DUKE

          Such freedom
Will not be good for him. We'll have him trained
For courtly merriment, for feasts and dancing.
Send him to me; and settle on your son
A livelihood in keeping with his station . . .
You frown – you're weary from the road, I think.

BARON

Not weary, sire; but out of countenance.
You force me, now, to tell you of my son
That which I could have wished you never knew.
My lord, he isn't worthy of your favour,
Of your concern: he wastes his youth in riot,
In vice . . .

THE DUKE

      He is too much alone; the young
Are harmed by idleness and solitude.

Send him to us: he'll soon forget the habits
Born of a life outside society.

BARON

I have to say, my lord, forgive me –
I truly can't agree to it . . .

THE DUKE

Why's that?

BARON

An old man begs your leave . . .

THE DUKE

I must demand
Your grounds.

BARON

My son displeases me.

THE DUKE

How so?

BARON

An evil crime . . .

THE DUKE

What has he done, this son?

BARON

My lord, I beg you . . .

THE DUKE

This is very strange –
Are you ashamed of him?

BARON

Indeed I am, sire.

THE DUKE

But tell me what it is he's done.

BARON

He wanted
To kill me.

THE DUKE

     Kill you! He'll be brought to court
For blackest villainy.

BARON

        My gracious lord –
I'll not give evidence, although it's plain
He wishes for my death – although he tried . . .
To . . .

THE DUKE

  What?

BARON

   To rob me!

Albert rushes into the room.

ALBERT

      Sir, you lie!

THE DUKE *(to Albert)*

            How dare you?

BARON

You here! You dare . . . address a father so!
I lie! Before our liege-lord! Am I not
A knight?

ALBERT

   A liar!

BARON

     Thunder never rolled
Till now! Just God – the sword shall be our judge!

Throws down a glove; his son at once picks it up.

ALBERT

This gift I thank you for: the first.

THE DUKE

           I see
A son take up his poor old father's challenge!
What times are these to wear the ducal chain!

Madman – young tiger!

(To the son)

Give the glove to me.

Takes the glove from Albert.

ALBERT (aside)

Too bad.

THE DUKE

How deep his claws have sunk! – Wild beast!

Out of my sight! And never dare come back
Until I summon you.

Exit Albert.

Shame on you, old man.

BARON

Forgive me, sire . . . I cannot stand . . . My knees
Are weak . . . I'm stifling . . . stifling . . . Ah my keys!
Where are my keys? . . .

THE DUKE

He's dead. Black times! Black hear

34

Mozart and Salieri

SCENE I

A room.

SALIERI

Justice, they say, does not exist on earth.
But justice won't be found in heaven either:
That's plain as any simple scale to me.
Born with a love of art, when as a child
I heard the lofty organ sound, I listened,
I listened and the sweet tears freely flowed.
Early in life I turned from vain amusements;
All studies that did not accord with music
I loathed, despised, rejected out of hand;
I gave myself to music. Hard as were
The earliest steps, and dull the earliest path,
I rose above reverses. Craftsmanship
I took to be the pedestal of art:
I made myself a craftsman, gave my fingers
Obedient, arid virtuosity,
My ear precision; killing sound, dissecting
Music as if it were a corpse, I checked
My harmony by algebra. At last,
Having achieved a mastery of theory,
I ventured on the rapture of creation.
I started to compose; in secrecy,
Not dreaming yet of glory. Many a time,
When I had sat in silence in my cell
Two days and more, forsaking sleep and food,
Tasting the bliss and pain of inspiration,
I burned my work and watched indifferently
As my ideas, the sounds I had created
Flared up and disappeared in wisps of smoke.
But what of that? For when the mighty Gluck
Revealed to us his new, enchanting secrets,
Did I not put behind me all I knew,
All that I loved, believed so fervently?
Did I not follow promptly in his path,
As trustful as a traveller redirected

By someone he encounters on the way?
Through zealous, unremitting application
I gained a not inconsequential place
In art's infinity. Fame smiled on me;
I found the hearts of men in harmony
With my creations. Happiness was mine;
My toil, success and glory I enjoyed
In peace – as too, success and fame of friends,
My fellows in the majesty of music.
I knew no envy – never! – not when first
I heard the opening of *Iphigenia*,
Not when Piccini tamed Parisian ears.
Who could have called the proud and free Salieri
A wretched envier, a trampled serpent
Alive yet helpless, biting sand and dust?
No-one! . . . But now – and *I* who say it – now
I envy – I profoundly envy. Heaven!
O where is justice when the sacred gift,
Immortal genius, comes not in reward
For toil, devotion, prayer, self-sacrifice –
But shines instead inside a madcap's skull,
An idle hooligan's? O Mozart, Mozart!

Enter Mozart.

MOZART

You've seen me! – Damn! I have a joke for you –
I wanted to surprise you.

SALIERI

You here . . .

MOZART

Yes,
I came to show you something: on my way
I passed an inn, and there I heard a fiddle . . .
A funnier sound you never heard, Salieri –
A blind old tavern fiddler's 'Voi che sapete'!
Priceless! I couldn't help myself; I've brought him
To entertain you with his art. Come in!

Enter a blind old man with a violin.

Something by Mozart, please.

The old man plays an aria from Don Giovanni;
Mozart roars with laughter.

SALIERI

How can you laugh?

MOZART

How can you *not* laugh? Oh Salieri!

SALIERI

No:
I'm not amused when some appalling dauber
Tries his Raphael Madonna out on me,
I'm not amused when wretched mountebanks
Dishonour Dante with their parodies.
Be off, old man.

MOZART

Wait – drink my health with this.

Exit old man.

You're out of sorts today, Salieri. Well,
I'll come another time.

SALIERI

What have you brought?

MOZART

Oh, nothing much. The other night insomnia
Plagued me again, some thoughts went through my head.
I wrote them down. I wanted your opinion . . .
You haven't time for me.

SALIERI

Oh Mozart! I –
No time for you? Sit down; I'm listening.

MOZART

At the piano.

Now,
Imagine . . . whom? – Myself, a little younger;
And I'm in love – not deeply, just a bit;

I'm with a pretty girl, or friend – say you,
I'm happy . . . Then: a vision of the grave,
Or sudden darkness, something of the kind.
Listen.

Plays.

SALIERI

　　　　You came to me with this, and stopped
To listen to a tavern scraper! Mozart,
You are unworthy of yourself.

MOZART

　　　　　　　　　You like it?

SALIERI

What grace! What depth – what bold magnificence!
Mozart, you are a god: you do not know it,
But I know, I know.

MOZART

　　　　　　　Nonsense! Well . . . who knows?
I'm starving though, in my divinity.

SALIERI

Let's dine together, come – The Golden Lion.

MOZART

Gladly. But first I'll have to tell my wife
I won't be home for supper.

Exit.

SALIERI

　　　　　　　　Don't forget . . .
I cannot bend the course of destiny –
For I am chosen, I must stop him now,
Or he will be the downfall of us all,
Us ministers and acolytes of music,
Not only me, of humble fame . . . What good
If Mozart should live on to reach new heights?
Will music be the better? Not at all;
Music will fall again, he'll leave no heir.
What use is he? He brings us, cherub-like,

Snatches of song from heaven, only to stir
Wingless desire in us poor sons of dust
And fly away . . . Then let him fly away!
The sooner he can spread his wings the better.
Here's poison, my Isora's dying gift,
Kept eighteen years upon me – years when often
My life has seemed a throbbing wound, when often
Some carefree foe and I have sat together,
And never have I yielded to temptation,
Though I'm no coward, though I feel a wrong
Most deeply, though I've little love for life.
When thirst for death tormented me, I waited;
I thought: Why should I die? For life, perhaps,
Will bring me new and unexpected gifts;
I shall be visited, perhaps, with rapture,
With inspiration and creative night;
Perhaps great works will come from some new Haydn
For my delight . . . In hated company
I thought: Perhaps I'll find far worse a foe,
Perhaps far worse a wrong will fall on me
From overbearing heights – and then I know,
Isora's precious gift, you will not fail.
And I was right! I've found my foe at last:
A second Haydn fills my soul with rapture!
The time has come now. Sacred gift of love,
Today the cup of friendship shall receive you!

SCENE II

Private room at an inn. A piano. Mozart
and Salieri are seated at table.

SALIERI

You sit so plunged in gloom.

MOZART

Me? Not at all.

SALIERI

Mozart – I never saw you so distracted:
A first-rate dinner, splendid wine – you're silent,
Frowning.

MOZART

My Requiem . . . it troubles me.

SALIERI

A Requiem? When did you start it?

MOZART

Oh,
Three weeks ago. But something very strange . . .
Didn't I tell you?

SALIERI

No.

MOZART

Well, listen now.
Three weeks ago I came home late at night.
Someone had called and asked for me – what for
I'd no idea. All night I thought – Who was it?
What can he want with me? The following day
The same man came again when I was out.
Next day my little boy and I were playing –
When I was called: a man in black – he bowed,
Ordered a Requiem, and disappeared.
I started work at once. And since that day
The man in black has never called again;
I'm glad – although the Requiem is finished
I shouldn't like to part with it. But . . .

SALIERI

What?

MOZART

I feel ashamed to tell you . . .

SALIERI

Tell me what?

MOZART

Everywhere, day and night, the man in black
Follows me like my shadow. Even now
It seems he's sitting here with us.

SALIERI

Enough!
What childish fears are these? Now Beaumarchais –
He used to say to me: 'My dear Salieri,
My remedy for gloomy thoughts: Either
Uncork a vintage bottle of champagne
Or reread *Figaro*.'

MOZART

Ah, Beaumarchais;
He used to be a friend of yours, I know.
You wrote *Tarare* for him – a glorious thing:
It has that tune . . . I sing it when I'm happy –
La la la la . . . Salieri, is it true,
Did Beaumarchais once really poison someone?

SALIERI

His cheerfulness would ill have fitted him
For such a trade.

MOZART

And then he is a genius,
Like you and me. Genius and evil-doing
Don't go together. Surely that is so?

SALIERI

You think so?

(To himself)
Now . . .

Drops poison into Mozart's glass.
Let's drink.

MOZART

Your health, my friend:
The bond that links us – Mozart and Salieri,
Two sons of harmony.

Drinks.

SALIERI

Wait – wait . . . You drank
Without me!

MOZART

(Tossing his napkin to the table)
There – enough.
Goes to the piano.
Listen, Salieri,
My Requiem.

Plays.
You weep?

SALIERI

Such tears as these
I've never shed: I feel both joy and pain,
As if acquitted of some grievous duty,
As if the healing knife had clean removed
A festering limb! Mozart, my friend, these tears . . .
Pay no attention. More, I beg of you,
Play on this moment, fill my soul with music . . .

MOZART

If only everyone so felt the power
Of harmony! Ah no, for then the world
Could not go on; life's needs would be neglected;
All would pursue the liberty of art.
We happy, idle chosen ones are few,
Who scorn utility, proud priests of beauty.
Not so? – I don't feel well – I'll go to bed.
Good-night!

SALIERI

Good-night.
(Alone)
Long will you sleep now, Mozart!
Can he be right? Genius and evil-doing

Don't go together; I am not a genius . . .
It isn't true: take Michelangelo;
Or was it just a rabble's rumour – was
The Vatican's creator no assassin?

The Stone Guest

LEPORELLO. O statua gentilissima
Del gran' Commendatore! . . .
. . . Ah, Padrone!

Don Giovanni

SCENE I

Don Juan and Leporello.

DON JUAN

Let's make a halt till dark. At last, Madrid!
I'll soon be striding through those streets again,
Hat over brow, moustaches tucked in cloak.
What would you say? Who's going to know it's me?

LEPORELLO

No easy task to recognise Don Juan!
I've seen a multitude like him!

DON JUAN

                                        You mean it?
Well, who on earth will know?

LEPORELLO

                                        The first nightwatchman,
Tipsy fiddler, or strolling gypsywoman –
Some other brazen cavalier like you,
Holding his sword inside well-mantled arm.

DON JUAN

No great misfortune if I'm recognised.
Only I mustn't meet the King . . . but then
There's no-one I'm afraid of in Madrid.

LEPORELLO

Listen – the King is sure to know tomorrow
Don Juan has returned without permission:
What will he do?

DON JUAN

                                        Send me away again.
I don't suppose I'll have my head chopped off.
I'm not accused of crime against the State;
The King still loved me when he banished me –
Purely to save me from the dead man's family.

LEPORELLO

Well then, you should have stayed in safety!

DON JUAN

Why,
I nearly died of boredom. What a people –
And what a countryside! The sky – pure smoke!
The women! No, my foolish Leporello,
I wouldn't for the life of me exchange
The ugliest Andalusian peasantwoman
For all the beauties of that place. At first
They dazzled me – their deep-blue eyes, their paleness,
Their modesty – or simply, novelty;
Thank God, I soon found out their worthlessness –
Lifeless creatures, nothing but waxen dolls;
Our beauties now! . . . You recognise this place?

LEPORELLO

Of course — Saint Antony's, the monastery
You used to visit; how could I not remember?
I used to mind the horses in that grove,
A thankless task. Your time was spent, believe me,
More happily than mine here.

DON JUAN

(pensively)

Poor Iñez!
She is no more . . . And how I loved her!

LEPORELLO

Yes,
Iñez the dark-eyed, I recall. Three months
It took – the Devil barely helped you there!

DON JUAN

Those evenings in July . . . A strange appeal
Her sad eyes held for me, her ashen lips.
To you she was no beauty, I remember.
Most strange . . . And little indeed there was about her
One might have reckoned beautiful. The eyes,
Only the eyes. Ah, such a gaze as hers
I'd never met before. And then her voice,
Quiet and faint, as if an invalid's, –

Her husband was a blackguard and a brute
I found out all too late . . . My poor Iñez!

LEPORELLO

What of it? After her came others.

DON JUAN

                              Yes.

LEPORELLO

And others, while we live, will follow.

DON JUAN

                                    True.

LEPORELLO

Well, now we're in Madrid – which one?

DON JUAN

                                    Laura!

I'll pay a call on her at once.

LEPORELLO

                    That's it.

DON JUAN

Anyone there – the window.

LEPORELLO

                    That's the style.

Now let's enjoy ourselves. Forget the dead.
Someone is coming – look.

Enter a monk.

MONK

                    This is the hour
She comes. Who's there? Not Doña Anna's people?

LEPORELLO

Not us, we're walking – by ourselves.

DON JUAN

                              Tell us –
Who is it you expect?

MONK

Why, Doña Anna;
This is her husband's graveside.

DON JUAN

Doña Anna
De Solva? Wife of the Comendador,
Killed by . . . I don't remember who . . .

MONK

A shameless,
Depraved and godless scoundrel named Don Juan.

LEPORELLO

So then! It seems Don Juan's reputation
Has even penetrated monasteries –
The holy sing his praises.

MONK

Do you know him?

LEPORELLO

Not in the least. Where is he now?

MONK

In exile.

LEPORELLO

Thank God for that. The further away the better.
Libertines! Bind them, gag them! Drown the lot!

DON JUAN

What slander –

LEPORELLO

Hush! I said all that on purpose . . .

DON JUAN

So – the Comendador is buried here?

MONK

Indeed. He lies beneath this monument
Erected by his widow; every day
She comes to mourn and pray here for his soul.

DON JUAN

Strange for a widow! Can she be good-looking?

MONK

A monk should not give thought to woman's charms,
But lying is sinful: beauty such as hers
Even a holy saint must recognise.

DON JUAN

No wonder the Comendador was jealous.
He kept his Doña Anna well locked up,
We none of us could get a glimpse of her.
What would I give to talk to her a little . . .

MONK

Oh, Doña Anna never talks to men.

DON JUAN

But father – you?

MONK

       That's different: I'm a monk.
Ah, here she is.

Enter Doña Anna.

DOÑA ANNA

Good father, let me in.

MONK

At once, Señora: I was waiting.

Doña Anna follows the monk.

LEPORELLO

       Well?
What do you think of her?

DON JUAN

       Invisible
Beneath those weeds – I glimpsed the tiniest heel.

LEPORELLO

Enough for you. Your swift imagination,
Defter than artist's pen, completes the picture;

To you it doesn't matter where you start:
The foot, the eyebrow.

DON JUAN

               Listen, Leporello,
I'll get to know her.

LEPORELLO

               So – he fells the husband
To watch the widow weep. That's him, my master!
Shameless!

DON JUAN

               It's dusk. Before the moon is up
And turns the shadows into brilliant light
We'll be inside Madrid.

LEPORELLO

               A Spanish noble
Waits like a thief for night and fears the moon –
What life is this! I'm truly sick of it.
How long, O Lord, until I'm rid of him?

SCENE II

Supper at Laura's house.

FIRST GUEST

You never played with such perfection, Laura,
So true an understanding of your role!

SECOND GUEST

Such art!

THIRD GUEST

               The power of your interpretation!

LAURA

Yes, I did well, in every word and gesture.
I freely gave myself to inspiration,

Today the speeches left my lips as if
Not servile memory, but the heart proclaimed them . . .

FIRST GUEST

And even now your eyes are shining, colour
Glows in your cheeks, the passion runs there still –
Let it not cool without a purpose, Laura:
Come, sing us something.

LAURA

Give me my guitar.

Sings.

ALL

Bravo! Bravo! Superb! Magnificent!

FIRST GUEST

Enchantress, you have charmed our hearts away.
Of life's enjoyments, music is surpassed
By love alone; but love is melody . . .
Your sullen Carlos – even he is moved.

SECOND GUEST

Ah what a song! Whose are the words?

LAURA

Don Juan's.

DON CARLOS

Don Juan's!

LAURA

Yes, some time ago he wrote them,
My faithful friend, my fickle paramour.

DON CARLOS

Don Juan is a scoundrel through and through,
And you – an imbecile.

LAURA

Have you gone mad?
I'll summon up my men this very moment,
I'll put you to the sword, grandee of Spain.

DON CARLOS

(Rises.)

Summon them, if you wish.

FIRST GUEST

I beg you, Laura –
Don Carlos, don't be angry. She forgot –

LAURA

That Juan, honourably in duel, despatched
Carlos's brother? Such a shame it wasn't
Carlos.

DON CARLOS

Fool that I was to lose my temper.

LAURA

Ah! he confesses. We'll be reconciled.

DON CARLOS

Forgive me, Laura – you must understand
I cannot hear that name indifferently.

LAURA

Am I to blame, I ask you, if my tongue
Happens upon that name from time to time?

GUEST

To prove your anger is forgotten, Laura,
Give us another song.

LAURA

Oh very well,
To say goodnight to you. It's dark already.
What shall I sing? . . . Listen.

Sings.

ALL

Charming! Superb!

LAURA

Goodnight, good gentlemen.

GUESTS

Goodnight, dear Laura.

They depart. Laura stops Don Carlos.

LAURA

Impetuous Carlos! Stay with me – you please me;
You made me think of Juan, cursing me
Through grinding teeth.

DON CARLOS

                Don Juan . . . Always lucky!
You loved him so.

LAURA

        Deeply.

DON CARLOS

          And still?

LAURA

              This moment?
No, two I cannot love. Now I love you.

DON CARLOS

Tell me, Laura – how old are you?

LAURA

            Eighteen.

DON CARLOS

You're young . . . five, six years more you will be young.
Men will gather about you six years more;
Flatter, caress you, shower you with their gifts,
Pay court to you in moonlight serenades,
At midnight crossroads kill each other for you.
But when your time is past, those eyes are hollow,
Those lids are shrunk, those tresses gleam with grey;
When you're accounted old – what then?

LAURA

              What then?
What talk is this? Why think such thoughts as these?
Do such things always occupy your mind?
Come out upon the balcony. How clear
The sky; the air is warm and still – the evening

Wafts us the scent of lemon-boughs and laurel;
The moon shines bright upon the deep dark blue –
The watchmen's long-drawn calls ring out: 'Calm night!' . . .
But somewhere in the distant north – in Paris –
Perhaps the sky is full of thunderclouds,
Rain falls, the chill wind blows . . . What's that to us?
Come now, my Carlos, I command – a smile!

DON CARLOS

Sweet demon!

Knocking is heard.

DON JUAN

Laura! Come!

LAURA

Whose voice is that?
Who's there?

DON JUAN

Open your door.

LAURA

It cannot be . . .

Opens the door; enter Don Juan.

O God!

DON JUAN

My love –

LAURA

Don Juan!

Throws herself upon his neck.

DON CARLOS

What! Don Juan!

DON JUAN

Laura, sweet love! . . .

Kisses her.

Who is your visitor?

DON CARLOS

Don Carlos.

DON JUAN

What an unexpected pleasure!
Tomorrow – at your service.

DON CARLOS

No! Now – here.

LAURA

This is my house, Don Carlos, not the street –
Leave us, I pray.

DON CARLOS

(not listening)

You have your sword. I'm waiting.

DON JUAN

Then as you wish; impatience shall be served.

They fight.

LAURA

No Juan! No!

Throws herself on the bed. Don Carlos falls.

DON JUAN

Laura, come now – it's over.

LAURA

What's this? He's dead? An excellent joke! In *my* house!
Now what am I to do, you ruffian – fiend?
Where shall I put him?

DON JUAN

Wait – perhaps he lives.

LAURA

Examines the body.

He lives! . . . Curse you! You've run him through the heart,
Clean through – no blood from this three-cornered wound,
He breathes no more – What have you got to say?

DON JUAN

He brought it on himself.

LAURA

How very tiresome.
That's my Don Juan: always up to mischief –
Never the guilty one . . . When did you get here?

DON JUAN

This evening, on the quiet – I'm not yet pardoned.

LAURA

No sooner in Madrid and thoughts of Laura?
How touching. Stuff and nonsense! Passing by
You chanced to recognise the house.

DON JUAN

Dear Laura,
Ask Leporello if I speak the truth.
I'm staying outside the town – some wretched inn . . .
And in Madrid for Laura.

Kisses her.

LAURA

O my love! . . .
No, wait – the corpse! What shall we do with it?

DON JUAN

Leave it for now. Before the crack of dawn
I'll take it out concealed beneath my cloak
And put it at a crossroads.

LAURA

Take good care
You're not observed. How very fortunate
You didn't come a moment sooner! Friends
Of yours were having supper here – they'd only
Just gone. If you'd come then!

DON JUAN

You've loved him long?

LAURA

Who do you mean? What reckless talk!

DON JUAN

Confess –
How often have you wantonly betrayed
Your exiled love?

LAURA

What about you, you rogue?

DON JUAN

Tell me . . . Not now, we'll talk about it later.

SCENE III

Tomb of the Comendador.

DON JUAN

All's for the best. Unlucky enough to kill
Don Carlos, taking refuge as a monk
Within these cloisters, every day I watch
My captivating widow, and in turn
I fancy she has noticed me. Till now –
Formalities. The time has come: today
I'll enter into conversation with her.
But how shall I begin? 'I make so bold' . . .
'Señora, pray' . . . What nonsense! I shall say
Whatever I think of, I can improvise
A lovesong . . . Time for her to come. Without her
I fear that our Comendador is bored.
The giant they've portrayed him in this statue!
Those shoulders! What a Hercules! In life
The late Comendador was small and frail;
He'd not have reached his statue's nose on tiptoe.
When we two met behind the Escorial
He ran at me, and on my outstretched sword
Froze like a dragonfly upon a pin, –

But bold and proud he was, and stern of soul . . .
Ah! Here she comes.

Enter Doña Anna.

DOÑA ANNA

The monk is here. Oh father,
I fear I interrupt your meditations –
Forgive me.

DON JUAN

I should surely ask forgiveness
Of you, Señora. I prevent, I fear,
The free unburdening of sorrow.

DOÑA ANNA

No,
My sorrow lies within me; in your presence
My humble prayers may rise to Heaven – Good father,
I beg you, join your voice with mine.

DON JUAN

I . . . pray . . .
With Doña Anna – pray! I am unworthy.
My unchaste lips shall not presume to speak
Your saintly prayer – My part to watch with reverence
While gracefully you bow your head and spill
Black hair on whitest marble – then it seems
An angel comes in secret to this tomb,
And in my wild and restless heart I find
No prayer, but silently I contemplate
The happy lot of him whose frigid marble
Is warmed thus with the breath of paradise,
And sprinkled with the tears of love . . .

DOÑA ANNA

How strange
Your words!

DON JUAN

Señora?

DOÑA ANNA

You've forgotten . . .

DON JUAN

                                 What?
That I'm a wretched monk, whose sinful voice
Should not be heard so loudly in this place?

DOÑA ANNA

I thought . . . I didn't understand . . .

DON JUAN

                            You know,
I see you know!

DOÑA ANNA

Know what?

DON JUAN

                    That I'm no monk –
Here at your feet I kneel and ask forgiveness.

DOÑA ANNA

O God have mercy! Rise, I beg . . . Who are you?

DON JUAN

The hopeless victim of an ill-starred passion.

DOÑA ANNA

O God! and here, beside this grave you speak!
Be gone.

DON JUAN

           I ask one moment, Doña Anna.

DOÑA ANNA

If someone comes!

DON JUAN

              The gate is closed. One moment!

DOÑA ANNA

Then – what do you want with me?

DON JUAN

                         O let me die
This instant at your feet – let my poor dust
Not rest beside this dust you hold so dear,

But further off – beneath the graveyard gate –
There you will touch my stone with gentle foot
Or garment, visiting this lordly tomb
To bow those locks and weep.

DOÑA ANNA
                    A madman speaks!

DON JUAN
To wish for death is madness, Doña Anna?
If I were mad, I'd wish to cling to life,
To bring your heart the soothing touch of love;
If I were mad, I'd watch beneath your window
Whole nights, keep you from sleep with serenades;
If I were mad, I'd place myself before you –
Not hide, not pine in silence . . .

DOÑA ANNA
                              This you call
Silence?

DON JUAN
        Believe me, Doña Anna, chance
Has lured me from my hiding – but for chance
You'd not have known the sorrow of my secret.

DOÑA ANNA
And have you loved me long?

DON JUAN
                          How long or lately
I cannot say. But since that love began
I've learned the price of every passing moment,
And what it means to speak of happiness.

DOÑA ANNA
A man of danger . . . Go.

DON JUAN
                    Danger?

DOÑA ANNA
                              I fear
Your words.

DON JUAN

                 Then I'll be silent: do not banish
A soul who takes no joy but in your sight.
I cherish no presumptuous hopes, I ask
Nothing, but if I am condemned to life
See you I must.

DOÑA ANNA

                 Be gone – here is no place
For speeches such as these. Come to my house
Tomorrow evening. Promise me respect,
And there I shall receive you; not too early –
I've not been in the way of company
In widowhood . . .

DON JUAN

                 O saintly Doña Anna!
May bounteous God grant you such consolation
As you have this poor sufferer today.

DOÑA ANNA

Go now.

DON JUAN

                 A moment more – I beg.

DOÑA ANNA

                                     It seems
Then – I must go . . . You've put my mind from prayer
With worldly speeches; long, how long ago
My ear grew unaccustomed to such words, –
Tomorrow I'll receive you.

DON JUAN

                              No, I cannot,
I dare not credit such a stroke of fortune . . .
Tomorrow I shall see you! – not in secret,
Not here!

DOÑA ANNA

         Tomorrow, yes indeed, tomorrow.
What is your name?

DON JUAN
Diego de Càlvado.

DOÑA ANNA
Until we meet, Don Diego.
Exit.

DON JUAN
Leporello!
Enter Leporello.

LEPORELLO
Your pleasure, sir?

DON JUAN
My Leporello! Oh,
I'm happy as a child! 'Tomorrow evening' –
Tomorrow, Leporello! – 'Not too early . . .'
Go and prepare . . .

LEPORELLO
You spoke to Doña Anna?
She said a kindly word to you . . . you blessed her?

DON JUAN
No, Leporello, no – an invitation!
From her – an invitation!

LEPORELLO
Invitation!
Oh widows! All the same.

DON JUAN
O happiness!
I want to sing out loud, embrace the world.

LEPORELLO
But what will the Comendador say now?

DON JUAN
You think he might be jealous? Surely not;
He'll not be such a hothead now he's dead.

LEPORELLO

I'm not so sure: look at his statue.

DON JUAN

Well?

LEPORELLO

It seems it's glaring angrily at you.

DON JUAN

Go up to it and ask it, Leporello,
To pay a call on me tomorrow evening –
That is, on Doña Anna.

LEPORELLO

Ask the statue!

Whatever for?

DON JUAN

Oh, not for conversation –
Ask it if it will come tomorrow evening
To Doña Anna's house – but not too early –
And stand on guard outside the door.

LEPORELLO

Take care

With whom you joke!

DON JUAN

You go and ask it.

LEPORELLO

I . . .

DON JUAN

Go on.

LEPORELLO

Most excellent and gracious statue –
My noble lord, Don Juan, humbly asks
If you will come . . . I can't – I'm terrified!

DON JUAN

Coward! Just wait . . .

LEPORELLO

No, no – I'll ask it now.
Noble Don Juan asks if you will come
Tomorrow evening to your spouse's house,
And stand outside the door . . . and . . .

The statue nods affirmatively.

DON JUAN

What's the matter?

LEPORELLO

The end has come!

DON JUAN

What is it?

LEPORELLO

(Nodding his head)

Ah . . . the statue!

DON JUAN

Why do you nod?

LEPORELLO

The statue nodded!

DON JUAN

Fool!

LEPORELLO

You speak to it.

DON JUAN

Watch me then, lily-liver.

(To the statue)

My good Comendador, tomorrow evening
Come to your widow's house – I shall be there–
And will you stand outside the door on guard?
You'll come?

The statue nods again.
The statue nods!

LEPORELLO

You see . . .

DON JUAN

Away!

SCENE IV

A room in Doña Anna's house.
Don Juan and Doña Anna.

DOÑA ANNA

I offer you my company, Don Diego;
I only fear a widow's gloomy talk
Will bore you. Still I feel my loss; like April
I mingle tears with smiles. Why are you silent?

DON JUAN

Dumb in the contemplation of my joy:
I am alone with Doña Anna, here,
Not at the fortunate departed's tomb –
For once, I see you not upon your knees
Before your marble spouse.

DOÑA ANNA

So jealousy
Pursues my husband in the grave, Don Diego?

DON JUAN

Jealous I cannot be. You chose him.

DOÑA ANNA

No,
My mother gave my hand to Don Alvaro.
Alvaro was a wealthy man.

DON JUAN

And lucky!
He laid before a goddess empty treasures,
And so, enjoys the bliss of Heaven! If only

I'd met you first – in what high exaltation
My rank, my wealth, my all would I have given,
All for a single glance of favour; slave
I should have been to your most sacred will,
How rapidly have read your merest whims,
Anticipated all, to make your life
One ceaseless moment of enchantment . . . No,
My destiny, alas! was otherwise.

DOÑA ANNA

Enough, I beg of you: I sin, Don Diego,
To listen to you – never can I love you,
A widow must be faithful to the grave.
If you had known Alvaro's love for me!
Alvaro, no! would never have received
A lady who professed her love for him
If he had lost a wife: he would have stayed
True to connubial love.

DON JUAN

                Do not torment me
By speaking of your husband, Doña Anna.
You've punished me enough, though punishment
I've brought upon myself, perhaps.

DOÑA ANNA

                       But how?
You are not bound, it seems, by sacred ties:
Your love for me is just, towards me, towards Heaven.

DON JUAN

Towards you! O God!

DOÑA ANNA

            I cannot think you've wronged me –
How so?

DON JUAN

     I cannot say.

DOÑA ANNA

           How strange, Don Diego:
But I demand you tell me.

DON JUAN

No, I cannot.

DOÑA ANNA

This then is your obedience to my will!
What did you say? You wished you were my slave!
You make me angry, Diego – answer me:
What have you done to wrong me?

DON JUAN

If I told you,
You'd hate me to your dying day.

DOÑA ANNA

I shall not –
I will forgive you here and now – for know
I must.

DON JUAN

But such a dark and murderous secret
Best you should never know.

DOÑA ANNA

You torture me . . .
A dark and murderous secret? What is this?
How could you injure me? I did not know you –
I have no enemies . . . I have but one:
My husband's murderer.

DON JUAN

(To himself)

Comes the revelation!

(To Doña Anna)

Tell me: that same unfortunate Don Juan –
You knew him, I suppose?

DOÑA ANNA

I never saw him.

DON JUAN

You foster hatred for him in your soul?

DOÑA ANNA

By honour's law. I think you try, Don Diego,
To turn me from my question. I demand . . .

68

DON JUAN

Were you to meet him now . . .

DOÑA ANNA

I'd plunge my dagger
Into the villain's heart.

DON JUAN

Then take your dagger –
Here is my heart.

DOÑA ANNA

Don Diego!

DON JUAN

I am Juan.

DOÑA ANNA

You lie.

DON JUAN

I killed your husband and I've no
Remorse.

DOÑA ANNA

What do I hear? It cannot be,
No, no!

DON JUAN

I am Don Juan and I love you.

DOÑA ANNA

(Falls)

I feel . . . I'm faint . . . Where am I?

DON JUAN

Doña Anna!
What ails you? Rise – collect yourself – Don Diego,
Your slave, is at your feet.

DOÑA ANNA

Leave me, I pray!

(Weakly)

You are my deadly foe – you took from me
All that I had . . .

DON JUAN

Incomparable creature!
I am resolved to expiate my deed:
Here at your feet I kneel to know your will –
I live or die for you . . .

DOÑA ANNA

This is Don Juan . . .

DON JUAN

Don Juan is described to you, no doubt,
As criminal and monster. – Doña Anna,
Maybe, report is not entirely false,
Maybe, upon a tried and weary conscience
There lies a weight of evil. Long was I
A model pupil of Debauchery;
O Doña Anna, since I saw you first
My inmost being has changed – in love with you
I am in love with virtue, and at last
On trembling knees I humbly bend before it.

DOÑA ANNA

Don Juan, well I know, is eloquent;
And also, I have heard, a sly seducer,
A godless libertine – a very demon.
How many helpless women have you ruined?

DON JUAN

None have I loved till now.

DOÑA ANNA

You'd have me think
I am the first Don Juan ever loved?
He doesn't seek one victim more in me?

DON JUAN

Had I in mind the purpose of deception,
Would I reveal myself, pronounce the name
You cannot bear to hear? What guile in this?

DOÑA ANNA

Who knows you – who could say? . . . How did you dare
Come here? If someone recognised you – death.

DON JUAN

And what is death? For one sweet hour with you
I'd give my life without a murmur.

DOÑA ANNA

But
So rashly here – how will you go unseen?

DON JUAN

(Kissing her hands)

You have a care for poor Don Juan's life!
Then Doña Anna's blessed soul contains
No hatred for me?

DOÑA ANNA

Would that I could hate you!
Now we must part.

DON JUAN

When shall we meet again?

DOÑA ANNA

I cannot say.

DON JUAN

Tomorrow?

DOÑA ANNA

Where?

DON JUAN

This house.

DOÑA ANNA

How weak I am of heart.

DON JUAN

One kiss of pardon . . .

DOÑA ANNA

You must be gone from here.

DON JUAN

One cool, cold kiss . . .

DOÑA ANNA

Oh how relentlessly you press! – Here then.
Who's knocking at the door? . . . Don Juan, hide.

DON JUAN

Goodbye, beloved.

Exit and comes running back.

Ah!

DOÑA ANNA

What is it? Ah! . . .

Enter the statue of the Comendador. Doña Anna faints.

STATUE

I come in answer to your invitation.

DON JUAN

O God, have mercy!

STATUE

Leave her. All is finished.

Don Juan trembles.

DON JUAN

No – I'm glad you've come.

STATUE

Give me your hand.

DON JUAN

How hard this clasp of stone!
Let me alone, let go – let go my hand . . .
I die – My end has come – O Doña Anna!

They sink out of sight.

The Feast during the Plague

From Wilson's tragedy *The City of the Plague*

A street. A table covered with glasses.
Carousing men and women.

YOUNG MAN

I rise to give, most noble President,
The memory of a man well known to all,
A man whose jest and merry anecdote,
Sharp repartee and witty epigram
(Most biting in its solemn gravity)
Livened our table, drove away the darkness
Our present visitor the Plague inflicts
Upon the brightest intellects among us.
But two days past, our laughter crowned his stories;
It cannot be, amid our merriment,
That Jackson is forgotten! Here his chair
Stands empty still, as if expecting back
The jovial wassailer – but now he keeps
A cold and subterranean abode . . .
Although the tongue of highest eloquence
Regales the dust of graves, still many of us
Remain among the living; we've no cause
For sorrowing. I give you, then, his memory,
With ringing goblets and with acclamation,
As if he lived.

MASTER OF REVELS

He was the first of us
To die. No, let us drink to him in silence.

YOUNG MAN

In silence, then!

All drink in silence.

MASTER OF REVELS

Your voice, dear Mary, gives us
The wild perfection of your native airs;
Sing us a song, come, sad and slow; and then
To merriment more madly than before,
As to the world of everyday from dreams.

MARY *(Sings)*

Once in this our country
    Peace and plenty ruled;
Once upon a Sunday
    Holy church was filled;
From the crowded school-house
    Children's voices pealed,
Busy scythe and sickle
    Sparkled in the field.

Church is now forsaken;
    School-house all forlorn;
Darkling grove is empty;
    Wasted is the corn;
Like a burnt-out building
    Stands each street of doom; –
All is still and silent
    Save the swelling tomb.

Always dead are carried;
    Groans of those that live
Peace to the departed
    Call on God to give.
Always room is needed;
    Graves of new-interred
Draw their ranks together
    Like some frightened herd.

Should my Spring be destined
    Early to the grave –
You whom once I loved so,
    All the joy life gave,
Pray shun Jenny's body,
    Do not come too near
Those dead lips, but follow
    From afar the bier.

Go then from this village;
    Find some resting-place,

Where your soul's affliction
  Might be granted grace.
When the Plague is over,
  Seek my dust anew;
In the vault of Heaven
  Jenny will be trùe.

MASTER OF REVELS

We thank you, Mary, for this plaintive song!
The Plague, it seems, came to your hills and valleys
Of old, and all along the banks of streams
That gambol now through that wild paradise
The sound of pitiful lament was heard;
The year that claimed the beautiful and brave
Has left us scarce a memory of itself
In simple sad-sweet pastoral song . . . This music
That echoes in the heart – nothing I know
Can bring such poignancy to merriment!

MARY

Would I had never sung to any ears
Except my parents' in our humble home!
They loved to have their Mary sing to them;
I seem to hear my singing from our threshold –
That maiden's voice was sweeter far; the voice
Of innocence . . .

LOUISA

                  This cant is out of fashion!
But simple souls there are still, quick to melt
At women's tears, and blindly credit them.
She really seems to think her tear-filled eyes
Quite irresistible – but if just now
She'd thought of laughter, she'd as soon have smiled.
Walsingham praises wailing northern beauties –
So up she starts her moaning. How I hate
Her yellow Scottish hair!

MASTER OF REVELS

                  Hush now! Listen –
I hear the sound of wheels.

A cart laden with dead passes by, driven by a Negro.

Louisa – fainted –
And by her tongue I'd thought her soul a man's.
The harsh, it seems, are weaker than the mild,
And abject fear inhabits passionate hearts!
Mary, a cup of water on her face.

MARY

Come, sister of my sorrow and my shame,
Lean on my breast.

LOUISA *(coming to)*

A black-faced, white-eyed demon
Beckoned me to his cart, piled high with corpses
That babbled some dread tongue . . . Was this a dream?
Or did the dead-cart pass?

YOUNG MAN

Courage, Louisa!
Although this street belongs to us alone,
Our haven from the ravages of death,
Where we may feast in peace – that cart will drive
Wherever it will, and we must let it pass!
Come, Walsingham: to put an end to quarrels
And female fainting fits – a song, a song!
A free and lively song I ask of you,
None of that tedious Scottish melancholy –
Let's have a roaring, bacchanalian song
Straight from the foam of flowing cups.

MASTER OF REVELS

I know none:
I'll sing a song to celebrate the Plague –
I wrote it when we'd parted yesterday.
I felt a strange and burning thirst for rhyme,
Unknown to me before! Listen: you'll find
The hoarseness of my voice most apt for song.

ALL

A song to celebrate the Plague! Let's hear it!
A song to celebrate the Plague! Bravo!

MASTER OF REVELS *(Sings)*

When great Winter he throws
　　At his obstinate foes
Shaggy legions of frost, ice and snow –
We meet them with feasting's glad glow.

　　The Black Queen with her hosts
　　A rich harvest she boasts,
And her spade raps our doors night and day . . .
What can we do now but pray?

　　Let us shut out the Plague
　　Like the Winter's rampage!
We'll carouse, and our goblets we'll drain
To the Plague's universal reign.

　　There's a savage delight
　　In the thick of the fight,
The chasm, the ocean's dark rage,
The whirlwind, the smell of the Plague.

　　In what threatens with death
　　Our mortal breath,
Should we make its discovery –
There is joy – immortality!

　　To the Plague then, all praise –
　　None her summons dismays!
Let us drink, while the cup overflows,
Of the breath of the Maid of the Rose!

Enter an old priest.

PRIEST

O godless feast! O godless libertines!
So to abuse the silence spread by death
In banqueting and song! Amid white faces
And lamentations of bereaved I pray –
While your excesses shake the graveyard's peace,

The very earth above the unsheeted dead!
Were not old men's and women's prayers to hallow
The wide and common grave, I could have thought
A horde of devils dragged an atheist's soul
To darkest depths with shouts of mocking laughter.

SEVERAL VOICES

How masterfully he speaks to us of hell!
Away, old man, away!

PRIEST

           Cease, I conjure you,
Upon the blood of Him who died for us:
Cease these abominations, if you'd meet
In heaven the loved ones you have lately lost –
Go to your homes!

MASTER OF REVELS

           Our homes are dismal places –
And youth loves gaiety.

PRIEST

           O Walsingham . . .
Three weeks ago you kissed your mother's corpse,
And wailing, threw yourself upon her grave . . .
You cannot think she's ceased to weep in Heaven
To see her son's unholy revelry,
To hear his voice upraised in frenzied song
'Mid sighs of grief and prayers of the devout?
Come, follow me!

MASTER OF REVELS

           Why seek to stop our feast?
I cannot go with you: here I am held
By hopelessness, dread memories of the past,
And knowledge of my depths of lawlessness,
And terror of the darkness of my home –
The novelty of unconfined delights,
The grateful poison of this brimful bowl,
The kisses (God forgive me) of this lost
But lovely creature . . . No, my mother's soul

Will never move me from this spot – too late –
I hear your voice that calls to me, to save me:
For this I thank you . . . Go in peace, old man;
But curst be any of us who follow you!

SEVERAL VOICES

Bravo, bravo, our noble President!
Father, a sermon for you there! Be off!

PRIEST

Matilda's sainted spirit calls on you!

MASTER OF REVELS *(Starts up)*

Swear to me now, your pale and withered hand
Lifted to heaven, to leave that silenced name
Forever in the grave! Would I could hide
This spectacle from her immortal eyes!
She thought me pure and proud and free, she found
Paradise in my arms . . . What am I now?
O holy child of light, I see you seated
Where my far-fallen soul can never rise!

FEMALE VOICE

Madman! He babbles of a buried wife!

PRIEST

Away, away . . .

MASTER OF REVELS

Father, for God's sake, leave me!

PRIEST

Almighty God have mercy on your soul!
Farewell, my son.

Exit priest. The feast continues.
The Master of Revels remains sunk in deep reverie.

80

Appendix

Pushkin's Original for *The Feast during the Plague*

John Wilson, *The City of the Plague* (1816),
Act I scene iv

The street. — A long table covered with glasses. — A party of
young men and women carousing.

YOUNG MAN

I rise to give, most noble President,
The memory of a man well known to all,
Who by keen jest, and merry anecdote,
Sharp repartee, and humorous remark
Most biting in its solemn gravity,
Much cheer'd our out-door table, and dispell'd
The fogs which this rude visitor the Plague
Oft breathed across the brightest intellect.
But two days past, our ready laughter chased
His various stories; and it cannot be
That we have in our gamesome revelries
Forgotten Harry Wentworth. His chair stands
Empty at your right hand – as if expecting
That jovial wassailer – but he is gone
Into cold narrow quarters. Well, I deem
The grave did never silence with its dust
A tongue more eloquent; but since 't is so,
And store of boon companions yet survive,
There is no reason to be sorrowful;
Therefore let us drink unto his memory
With acclamation, and a merry peal
Such as in life he loved.

MASTER OF REVELS
'T is the first death
Hath been amongst us, therefore let us drink
His memory in silence.

YOUNG MAN
Be it so.

They all rise, and drink their glasses in silence.

MASTER OF REVELS

Sweet Mary Gray! Thou hast a silver voice,
And wildly to thy native melodies
Can tune its flute-like breath – sing us a slong,
And let it be, even 'mid our merriment,
Most sad, most slow, that when its music dies,
We may address ourselves to revelry,
More passionate from the calm, as men leap up
To this world's business from some heavenly dream.

MARY GRAY'S SONG

I walk'd by mysel' ower the sweet braes o' Yarrow,
    When the earth wi' the gowans o' July was drest;
But the sang o' the bonny burn sounded like sorrow,
    Round ilka house cauld as a last simmer's nest.

I look'd through the lift o' the blue smiling morning,
    But never ae wee cloud o' mist could I see
On its way up to heaven, the cottage adorning,
    Hanging white ower the green o' its sheltering tree.

By the outside I ken'd that the inn was forsaken,
    That nae tread o' footsteps was heard on the floor;
– O loud craw'd the cock whare was nane to awaken,
    And the wild-raven croak'd on the seat by the door!

Sic silence – sic lonesomeness, oh, were bewildering!
    I heard nae lass singing when herding her sheep;
I met nae bright garlands o' wee rosy children
    Dancing on to the school-house just waken'd frae sleep.

I pass'd by the school-house – when strangers were coming,
    Whose windows with glad faces seem'd all alive;
Ae moment I hearken'd, but heard nae sweet humming,
    For a night o' dark vapour can silence the hive.

I pass'd by the pool where the lasses at daw'ing
    Used to bleach their white garments wi' daffin and din;
But the foam in the silence o' nature was fa'ing,
    And nae laughing rose loud through the roar of the linn.

I gaed into a small town – when sick o' my roaming –
    Whare ance play'd the viol, the tabor, and flute;
'T was the hour loved by Labour, the saft smiling gloaming,
    Yet the green round the Cross-stane was empty and mute.

To the yellow-flower'd meadow, and scant rigs o' tillage,
    The sheep a' neglected had come frae the glen;
The cushat-dow doo'd in the midst o' the village,
    And the swallow had flown to the dwellings o' men!

– Sweet Denholm! not thus, when I lived in thy bosom,
    Thy heart lay so still the last night o' the week;
Then nane was sae weary that love would nae rouse him,
    And Grief gaed to dance with a laugh on his cheek.

Sic thoughts wet my een – as the moonshine was beaming
    On the kirk-tower that rose up sae silent and white;
The wan ghastly light on the dial was streaming,
    But the still finger tauld not the hour of the night.

The mirk-time pass'd slowly in siching and weeping,
    I waken'd, and nature lay silent in mirth;
Ower a' holy Scotland the Sabbath was sleeping,
    And Heaven in beauty came down on the earth.

The morning smiled on – but nae kirk-bell was ringing,
    Nae plaid or blue bonnet came down frae the hill;
The kirk-door was shut, but nae psalm tune was singing,
    And I miss'd the wee voices sae sweet and sae shrill.

I look'd ower the quiet o' Death's empty dwelling,
    The lav'rock walk'd mute 'mid the sorrowful scene,
And fifty brown hillocks wi' fresh mould were swelling
    Ower the kirk-yard o' Denholm, last simmer sae green.

The infant had died at the breast o' its mither;
    The cradle stood still at the mitherless bed;
At play the bairn sunk in the hand o' its brither;
    At the fauld on the mountain the shepherd lay dead.

Oh! in spring-time 't is eerie, when winter is over,
    And birds should be glinting ower forest and lea,

When the lint-white and mavis the yellow leaves cover,
    And nae blackbird sings loud frae the tap o' his tree.

But eerier far, when the spring-land rejoices,
    And laughs back to heaven with gratitude bright,
To hearken! and naewhere hear sweet human voices!
    When man's soul is dark in the season o' light!

MASTER OF REVELS

We thank thee, sweet one! for thy mournful song.
It seems, in the olden time, this very Plague
Visited thy hills and valleys, and the voice
Of lamentation wail'd along the streams
That now flow on through their wild paradise,
Murmuring their songs of joy. All that survive
In memory of that melancholy year,
When died so many brave and beautiful,
Are some sweet mournful airs, some shepherd's lay
Most touching in simplicity, and none
Fitter to make one sad amid his mirth
Than the tune yet faintly singing through our souls.

MARY GRAY

O! that I ne'er had sung it but at home
Unto my aged parents! to whose ear
Their Mary's tones were always musical.
I hear my own self singing o'er the moor,
Beside my native cottage, – most unlike
The voice which Edward Walsingham has praised,
It is the angel-voice of innocence.

SECOND WOMAN

I thought this cant were out of fashion now.
But it is well; there are some simple souls,
Even yet, who melt at a frail maiden's tears,
And give her credit for sincerity.
She thinks her eyes quite killing while she weeps.
Thought she as well of smiles, her lips would pout
With a perpetual simper. Walsingham
Hath praised these crying beauties of the north,
So whimpering is the fashion. How I hate
The dim dull yellow of that Scottish hair!

MASTER OF REVELS

Hush! hush! – is that the sound of wheels I hear?

The Dead-cart passes by, driven by a Negro.

Ha! dost thou faint, Louisa! one had thought
That railing tongue bespoke a mannish heart.
But so it ever is. The violent
Are weaker than the mild, and abject fear
Dwells in the heart of passion. Mary Gray,
Throw water on her face. She now revives.

MARY GRAY

O sister of my sorrow and my shame!
Lean on my bosom. Sick must be your heart
After a fainting-fit so like to death.

LOUISA *(recovering)*

I saw a horrid demon in my dream!
With sable visage and white-glaring eyes,
He beckon'd on me to ascend a cart
Fill'd with dead bodies, muttering all the while
An unknown language of most dreadful sounds.
What matters it? I see it was a dream.
– Pray, did the dead-cart pass?

YOUNG MAN

                  Come, brighten up,
Louisa! Though this Street be all our own,
A silent street that we from death have rented,
Where we may hold our orgies undisturb'd,
You know those rumbling wheels are privileged,
And we must bide the nuisance. Walsingham,
To put an end to bickering, and these fits
Of fainting that proceed from female vapours,
Give us a song; – a free and gladsome song;
None of those Scottish ditties framed of sighs,
But a true English Bacchanalian song,
By toper chaunted o'er the flowing bowl.

MASTER OF REVELS

I have none such; but I will sing a song
Upon the Plague. I made the words last night,
After we parted: a strange rhyming-fit
Fell on me; 't was the first time in my life.
But you shall have it, though my vile cracked voice
Won't mend the matter much.

> A song on the Plague!
> A song on the Plague! Let's have it! bravo! bravo!

SONG

Two navies meet upon the waves
That round them yawn like op'ning graves;
The battle rages; seamen fall,
And overboard go one and all!
The wounded with the dead are gone;
But Ocean drowns each frantic groan,
And, at each plunge into the flood,
Grimly the billow laughs with blood.
– Then, what although our Plague destroy
Seaman and landman, woman, boy?
When the pillow rests beneath the head,
Like sleep he comes, and strikes us dead.
What though into yon Pit we go,
Descending fast, as flakes of snow?
What matters body without breath?
No groan disturbs that hold of death.

CHORUS

Then, leaning on his snow-white breast,
I sing the praises of the Pest!
If me thou wouldst this night destroy,
Come, smite me in the arms of Joy.

Two armies meet upon the hill;
They part, and all again is still.
No! thrice ten thousand men are lying,
Of cold, and thirst, and hunger dying.
While the wounded soldier rests his head
About to die upon the dead,
What shrieks salute yon dawning light?
'Tis Fire that comes to aid the Fight!
– All whom our Plague destroys by day,
His chariot drives by night away;
And sometimes o'er a churchyard wall
His banner hangs, a sable pall!
Where in the light by Hecate shed
With grisly smile he counts the dead,

And piles them up a trophy high
In honour of his victory.
   Then, leaning, etc.

King of the aisle! and churchyard cell!
Thy regal robes become thee well,
With yellow spots, like lurid stars
Prophetic of throne-shattering wars,
Bespangled in its night-like gloom,
As it sweeps the cold damp from the tomb.
Thy hand doth grasp no needless dart,
One finger-touch benumbs the heart.
If thy stubborn victim will not die,
Thou roll'st around thy bloodshot eye,
And Madness leaping in his chain
With giant buffet smites the brain,
Or Idiocy with drivelling laugh
Holds out her strong-drugg'd bowl to quaff,
And down the drunken wretch doth lie
Unsheeted in the cemetery.
   Then, leaning, etc.

Thou! Spirit of the burning breath,
Alone deservest the name of Death!
Hide, Fever! hide thy scarlet brow;
Nine days thou liger'st o'er thy blow,
Till the leech bring water from the spring,
And scare thee off on drenched wing.
Consumption! waste away at will!
In warmer climes thou fail'st to kill,
And rosy Health is laughing loud
As off thou steal'st with empty shroud!
Ha! blundering Palsy! thou art chill!
But half the man is living still;
One arm, one leg, one cheek, one side
In antic guise thy wrath deride.
But who may 'gainst thy power rebel,
King of the aisle! and churchyard cell!
   Then, leaning, etc.

To Thee, O Plague! I pour my song,
Since thou art come I wish thee long!

Thou strikest the lawyer 'mid his lies,
The priest 'mid his hypocrisies.
The miser sickens at his hoard,
And the gold leaps to its rightful lord.
The husband, now no longer tied,
May wed a new and blushing bride,
And many a widow slyly weeps
O'er the grave where her old dotard sleeps,
While love shines through her moisten'd eye
On yon tall stripling gliding by.
'T is ours who bloom in vernal years
To dry the love-sick maiden's tears,
Who turning from the relics cold,
In a new swain forgets the old.
                    Then, leaning, etc.

Enter an old grey-headed Priest.

O impious table! spread by impious hands!
Mocking with feast and song and revelry
The silent air of death that hangs above it,
A canopy more dismal than the Pall!
Amid the churchyard darkness as I stood
Beside a dire interment, circled round
By the white ghastly faces of despair,
That hideous merriment disturb'd the grave,
And with a sacrilegious violence
Shook down the crumbling earth upon the bodies
Of the unsheeted dead. But that the prayers
Of holy age and female piety
Did sanctify that wide and common grave,
I could have thought that hell's exulting fiends
With shouts of devilish laughter dragg'd away
Some harden'd atheist's soul unto perdition.

SEVERAL VOICES

How well he talks of hell! Go on, old boy!
The devil pays his tithes – yet he abuses him.

PRIEST

Cease, I conjure you, by the blessed blood
Of Him who died for us upon the Cross,
These most unnatural orgies. As ye hope
To meet in heaven the souls of them ye loved,

Destroy'd so mournfully before your eyes,
Unto your homes depart.

MASTER OF REVELS

Our homes are dull –
And youth loves mirth.

PRIEST

O, Edward Walsingham!
Art thou that groaning pale-faced man of tears
Who three weeks since knelt by thy mother's corpse,
And kiss'd the solder'd coffin, and leapt down
With rage-like grief into the burial vault,
Crying upon its stone to cover thee
From this dim darken'd world? Would she not weep,
Weep even in heaven, could she behold her son
Presiding o'er unholy revellers,
And tuning that sweet voice to frantic songs
That should ascend unto the throne of grace
'Mid sob-broken words of prayer!

YOUNG MAN

Why! we can pray
Without a priest – pray long and fervently
Over the brimming bowl. Hand him a glass.

MASTER OF REVELS

Treat his grey hairs with reverence.

PRIEST

Wretched boy!
This white head must not sue to thee in vain!
Come with the guardian of thy infancy,
And by the hymns and psalms of holy men
Lamenting for their sins, we will assuage
This fearful mirth akin to agony,
And in its stead, serene as the hush'd face
Of thy dear sainted parent, kindle hope
And heavenly resignation. Come with me.

YOUNG MAN

They have a design against the hundredth Psalm.
Oh! Walsingham will murder cruelly
'All people that on earth do dwell.'
Suppose we sing it here – I know the drawl.

MASTER OF REVELS

(silencing him, and addressing the Priest)

Why camest thou hither to disturb me thus?
I may not, must not go! Here am I held
By hopelessness in dark futurity,
By dire remembrance of the past, – by hatred
And deep contempt of my own worthless self, –
By fear and horror of the lifelessness
That reigns throughout my dwelling, – by the new
And frantic love of loud-tongued revelry, –
By the blest poison mantling in this bowl, –
And, help me Heaven! by the soft balmy kisses
Of this lost creature, lost, but beautiful
Even in her sin; nor could my mother's ghost
Frighten me from this fair bosom. 'Tis too late!
I hear thy warning voice – I know it strives
To save me from perdition, body and soul.
Beloved old man, go thy way in peace,
But curst be these feet if they do follow thee.

SEVERAL VOICES

Bravo! Bravissimo! Our noble president!
Done with that sermonizing – off – off – off!

PRIEST

Matilda's sainted spirit calls on thee!

MASTER OF REVELS

(starting distractedly from his seat)

Didst thou not swear, with thy pale wither'd hands
Lifted to Heaven, to let that doleful name
Lie silent in the tomb for evermore?
O that a wall of darkness hid this sight
From her immortal eyes! She, my betrothed,
Once thought my spirit lofty, pure, and free,
And on my bosom felt herself in Heaven.
What am I now? *(looking up.)* – O holy child of light,
I see thee sitting where my fallen nature
Can never hope to soar!

FEMALE VOICE

        The fit is on him.
Fool! thus to rave about a buried wife!
See! how his eyes are fix'd.

MASTER OF REVELS
                    Most glorious star!
Thou art the spirit of that bright Innocent!
And there thou shinest with upbraiding beauty
On him whose soul hath thrown at last away
Not the hope only, but the wish of Heaven.

PRIEST
Come, Walsingham!

MASTER OF REVELS
                    O holy father! go.
For mercy's sake, leave me to my despair.

PRIEST
Heaven pity my dear son. Farewell! farewell!

The Priest walks mournfully away.

. . .

Notes

Page 19: *The Miserly Knight*. Completed 23 October 1830.

Page 35: *Mozart and Salieri*. Completed 26 October 1830.

Page 42: Salieri: 'His cheerfulness would ill have fitted him/ For such a trade.' The author of *The Barber of Seville* and *The Marriage of Figaro* actually led a dangerous political life. He undertook secret service missions for Louis XV and Louis XVI, and during the Revolution was an agent for the Committee of Public Safety. He survived the Terror through constant vicissitudes.

Page 44: Salieri: ' . . . Michelangelo . . .'. A reference to the legend that Michelangelo killed the model for his 'Crucifixion' in order to obtain greater realism.

Page 45: *The Stone Guest*. Completed 4 November 1830.
In this version names ending in a consonant are stressed on the last syllable, following the rules of Spanish pronunciation. But 'Juan' is anglicised to stress on the first syllable, in accordance with English literary tradition.

Page 52: First Guest: 'Of life's enjoyments, music is surpassed/ By love alone; but love is melody . . .' Pushkin inscribed these lines in 1828 in an album of the Polish pianist Szymanowska.

Page 54: Laura: '. . . cursing me/ Through grinding teeth.' Typically, the sound of the Russian conveys far more than any English rendering of sense: *'I stisnul zuby s skrezhetom.'* ('And clenched your teeth with a grinding.')

Page 57: Don Juan: 'And put it at a crossroads.' See page 54, Don Carlos: 'At midnight crossroads kill each other for you.'

Page 61: Don Juan: 'How long or lately . . . to speak of happiness.' F. F. Seeley ('The Problem of *Kamennyy Gost'*, *Slavonic and East European Review*, XLI, 97, June 1963, page 356) singles out these lines of Don Juan's as his most sincere so far in this scene with Doña Anna: 'a response of winning simplicity which comes closer to ringing true than anything that he has yet said to her'.

Page 66: Doña Anna: 'Still I feel my loss; like April/ I mingle tears with smiles.' As V. Terras has pointed out (Introduction to

Little Tragedies (in Russian), Bradda Books, Letchworth, 1966), here is an echo from Barry Cornwall's 'Dramatic Scene' *Ludovico Sforza*: '. . . Even I, you see,/ Although a widow, not divested of/ Her sorrows quite, am here i' the midst of tears,/ To smile, like April, on you . . .'

Page 72: Doña Anna: 'Oh how relentlessly you press! – Here then.' A high-point of the action.

Page 72: *'They sink out of sight.'* i.e. the Statue and Don Juan.

Page 73: *The Feast during the Plague.* Pushkin completed his translation on 6 November 1830. For a detailed comparison of his version with his source, see Henry Gifford, 'Pushkin's *Feast in time of Plague* and its Original', *American Slavic and East European Review*, VIII, 1949.

Page 74: Young Man: 'Although the tongue of highest eloquence/ Regales the dust of graves . . .' Pushkin 'mistranslates' Wilson's 'The grave did never silence with its dust/ A tongue more eloquent . . .'

Page 77: In Louisa's lines in Wilson, the demon is the subject of the verb 'babbled' ('muttering' in Wilson).

Page 77: Master of Revels: '. . . you'll find/ The hoarseness of my voice most apt for song.' Pushkin amends Wilson's 'though my vile crack'd voice/ Won't mend the matter much.' This is typical of his amendments of Wilson.

Page 91: *'The Priest walks mournfully away.'* Wilson's scene continues for another 90 lines or so, with Walsingham a moment later turning to the prostitute Mary: '. . . with a calm deliberate soul/ I swear to love thee!'